Home FUN booklet 3

T0363848

Jane Ritter

Letter to parents

Dear parents,

Welcome to *The Home Fun Booklet*! We hope you will use the activities inside to help your child practise English at home and with their friends.

Your child will bring home this booklet to practise with you what they have learned in class. You don't need to be an English expert to help your child with these activities. All the answers and audio recordings are online at http://www.cambridge.org/funresources . Have fun and keep practising with your child. Try to use the vocabulary here in everyday life and games and don't worry about making mistakes. On pages 7, 11, 15, 19 and 23 you will see this tree:

This tree shows how your child's knowledge will grow and progress through the units. Ask your child to read the 'I can…' sentences in the tree and to think about what they say. They can colour in the leaves green, orange or red when they agree – try to say 'Well done!'

The *Let's have fun!* pages (24–25) feature projects that develop language, mathematical, digital, social, learning and cultural skills useful for modern life. Look for the following signs next to activities in the booklet to show which of these skills your child is developing:

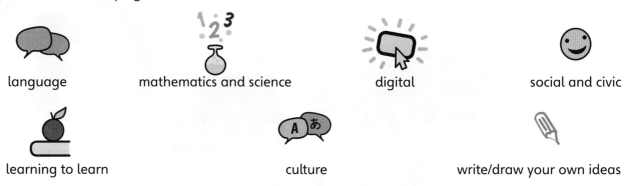

| language | mathematics and science | digital | social and civic |

| learning to learn | culture | write/draw your own ideas |

The picture dictionary at the end of the booklet (pages 26–31) is for your child to write in through the year. Ask them to write the words they know from all the topics. Make sure they can see they are progressing!

This booklet helps to prepare children for the Cambridge English: Young Learners tests, which are a great way to give your child more confidence in English and reward their learning. For more information, please go to: http://www.cambridgeenglish.org/exams/young-learners-english .

We hope both you and your child enjoy using this booklet and have fun!

The Cambridge Team

Download

the Word FUN World app

Contents

Jane Ritter

Animals

snail

skateboard

A **What's the first letter? Write and draw the animals.**

1

<u>s</u>   <u>h</u>   a   <u>r</u>   <u>k</u>   ....shark....

2

__   u   __   __   y   ....

3

w   __   a   __   __   ....

4

__   i   __   a   __   __   __   ....

B **Fun at home** **Look at the animals in A again. Close your eyes. How many can you say?**

There is an elephant, a snail, and a shark.

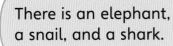

Jack can say .....3..... animals.

I can say .... animals.

Try again. How many can you say now?

I can say .... animals now.

4

C Look at the animals and the food. Count and colour.

8								
7								
6								
5								
4								
3								
2								
1								
0	penguins	pies	milkshakes	elephants	zebras	giraffes	bats	burgers

D Read and write.

1. How many pies and burgers are there?   ...1+3=4...
2. How many bats and penguins are there?   ....
3. How many milkshakes and elephants are there?   ....
4. How many zebras, elephants and giraffes are there?   ....
5. ....

How many penguins and giraffes are there?

There are ten.

How many meat and potato pies are there?

There is one.

5

Places

A Look and write *a, e, i, o, u*. Then say the words.

1
Funfair!
f _ n f _ _ r

2
c _ r c _ s

3
p l _ _ y g r _ _ _ n d

4
c _ r p _ r k

5
t _ w n c _ n t r _

6
c _ k _ s h _ p

B Read and draw lines.

1 You go there when you want to get on a train.

2 You can watch films with your family and friends here.

3 You can look at lots of books and buy them in this place.

 hospital

 cinema

supermarket

bookshop

station

5 You buy food and drinks and things for your home in this very big shop.

6 You go to this big building when you are very sick.

6

C Write and draw lines.

cake   dirty   ~~moon~~   penguin   thirsty

1

I want to go to the ....moon....... !

Shall I get you some lemonade?

2

My .... is hungry!

Shall I buy some eggs?

3

It's too hot. I'm really .... !

Shall I take you for a ride in my spaceship?

4

My bike is very ....

Shall I get some fish for your penguin?

5

I want to make a ....

Shall I help you wash it?

I know .... animal words.

✔ I can add numbers.

I can ask 'how many ...?' and answer 'there is ...' and 'there are ...'.

I know places in the town.

I can ask 'shall I ...?

= 😊

= 😐

= 🙁

The home

A ▶ **Listen and number 1–6.**
2

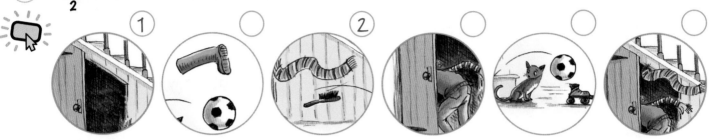

B Read and draw.

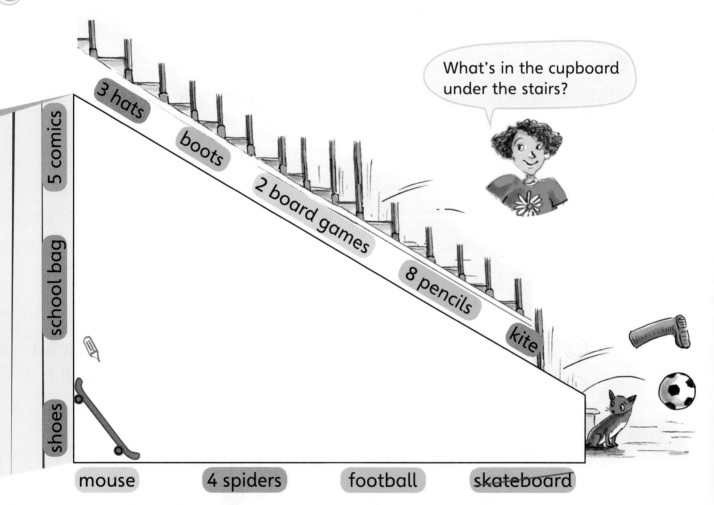

What's in the cupboard under the stairs?

5 comics

3 hats

boots

school bag

2 board games

8 pencils

kite

shoes

mouse   4 spiders   football   skateboard

C Tell your family about your picture.

The pencils are between the ball and the school bag.

The mouse is behind the boots.

The skateboard is by the door.

D **Look and write.**

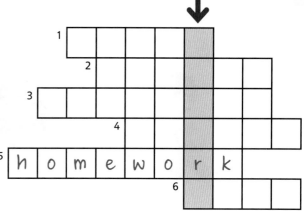

Meg looked under the ....

5 | h | o | m | e | w | o | r | k

E **Read and write *and*, *but* or *because*.**

My favourite room is the kitchen. My kitchen is very big. We eat in the
kitchen ....*because*.... we like it. There is a table, a chair .... lots
of food. The walls are blue .... it's my mum's favourite colour. I
like blue too .... my favourite colour is yellow.

F **Fun at home** **Look and say. Then draw the same room with 5
differences. Ask your family to find the differences.**

There is a ......*guitar*...... by the door.
There is a .... on the wall.

Sports and leisure

Look and write.

1

allbabse

.....baseball....

2

ncndaig

....

3

kyohce

....

4

tobanmind

....

5

rseoh dirgni

....

6

cei skingat

....

7

llrero tikagns

....

8

bardoskingate

....

B **Read and write.**

My name is Zoe.
I love going to school because we play a lot of sport.
I play in the school hockey team. My friends think I am very good at it. I play three times a week and I play a game on Saturdays too.
I like watching baseball on TV with my mum and dad. I have lessons at school but I'm terrible. I like baseball but I can't play it because I'm not good at throwing.
I want to try horse riding because I really like horses.

1 Zoe loves going to ....

2 She plays .... three times a week.

3 She enjoys .... baseball.

4 She isn't good at ....

5 She would like to go ....

C ▶ Listen and circle the words.
3

band

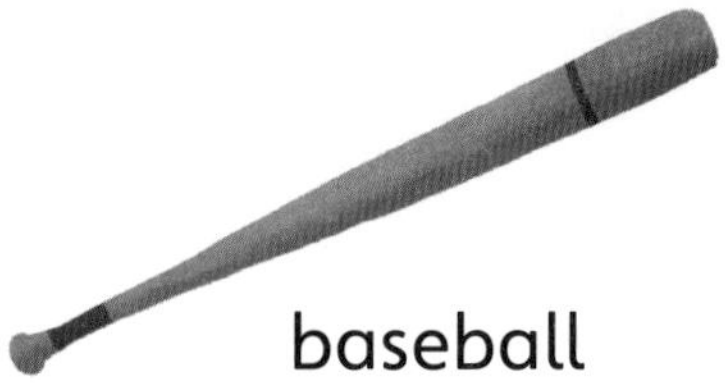

baseball

dancing

guitar

ice hockey

roller skating

soccer

D ▶ Listen again and write (✔) or (✖).
4

1. Fred has a blue baseball cap. ☐
2. Charlie is good at soccer. ☐
3. Fred and Charlie got four goals. ☐
4. Fred plays the piano. ☐
5. Charlie can sing. ☐

I can talk about my home.

I can say where things are in the home.

= ☺

= 😐

= ☹

I can use 'and', 'but' and 'because'.

I can read and write about sports.

I can listen to people talking about sports.

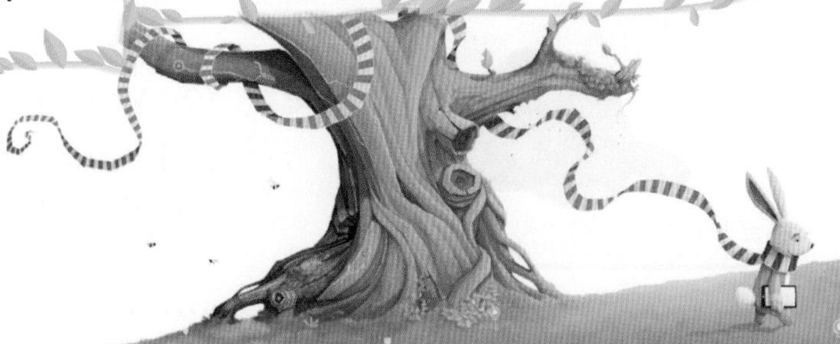

Review

A Read and write.

badminton	cake	~~chair~~	cheese	cinema
~~circus~~	cupboard	~~elephant~~	funfair	giraffe
ice skating	lemonade	~~meat and potato pie~~	~~milkshake~~
penguin	~~skateboarding~~	table	water

1 drinks
...milkshake...
....
....

2 food
...meat and potato pie...
....
....

3 places
......circus......
....
....

4 home
......chair......
....
....

5 animals
...elephant...
....
....

6 sports
skateboarding
....
....

B Read and write.

1 It's a sport. There are eleven people in each team. They use sticks and a small ball to play this sport. It's .....hockey..... .

2 It's small. It lives in the garden. It hasn't got any legs. It eats leaves. It can't run. It's a ....

3 You wear this on your head when you play sport in the sun. It's a ....

4 ....
....

C Read and colour.

horse	skating
town	park
car	station
polar	cap
roller	riding
bus	bear
baseball	centre

D Read and write.

Tom Age 10

My favourite sport is baseball.

It's fun and exciting.

I am good at throwing.

I play with my sister.

My favourite sport is ....

It's ....

I am ....

I ....

Family

A Look and write.

| aunt | brother | father | grandfather | ~~grandmother~~ | mother | uncle |

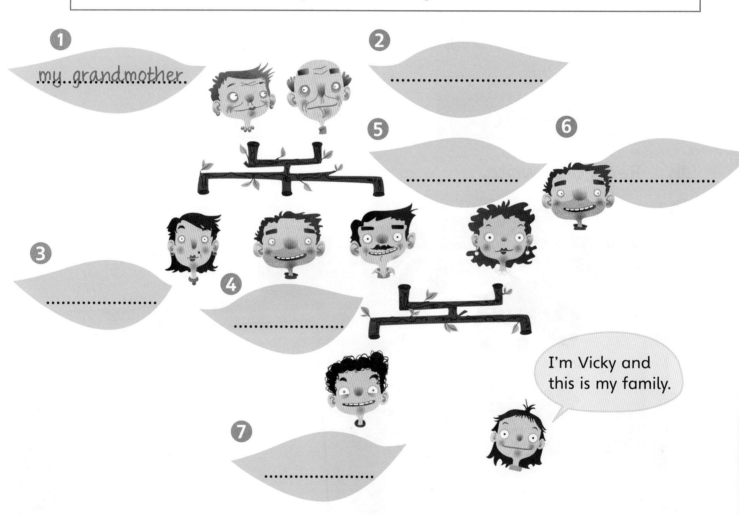

1 my grandmother

2 ....

5 ....

6 ....

3 ....

4 ....

7 ....

I'm Vicky and this is my family.

B How many words can you make? You can use the letters more than once.

Vicky's brother puts lots of pictures of monsters on his walls.

..........hockey.......... ....

..........upstairs.......... ....

....

14

C **Draw lines and write.**

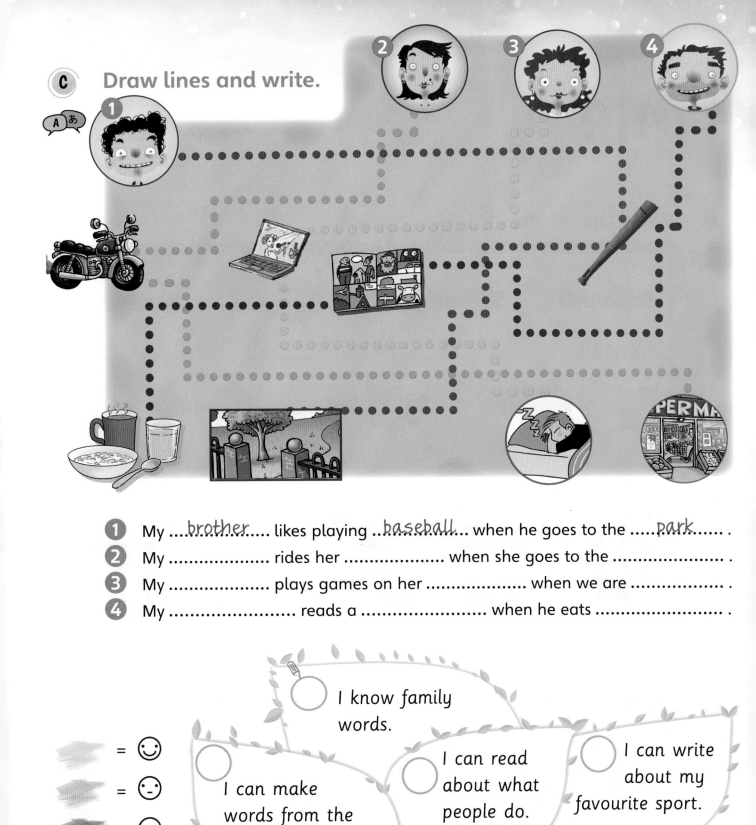

1 My ....brother.... likes playing ..baseball.. when he goes to the .....park...... .
2 My .... rides her .... when she goes to the ....
3 My .... plays games on her .... when we are ....
4 My .... reads a .... when he eats ....

= ☺
= 😐
= ☹

I know family words.

I can make words from the letters in a sentence.

I can read about what people do.

I can write about my favourite sport.

Time

A **Write the words.**

M**n**da**y** T**u**sd**a**y Wed**nes**day T**u**e**s**day

..Monday.... ....

>> ......**day** Sa**tur**day ....**nda**y

....

B **Look and write.**

1  **2**  **3**  **4** **5**

..It's..seven. ....
...o'clock..... ....

C **Read and draw.**

It's four o'clock.

It's six o'clock.

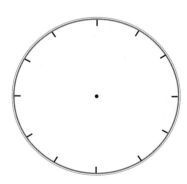

It's nine o'clock.

D **Tell your family what you do.**

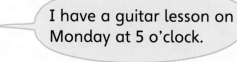

I have a guitar lesson on Monday at 5 o'clock.

I play badminton on Friday at 12 o'clock.

16

○ = ...e...
⬠ = ...
☆ = ...
▢ = ...
△ = ...

E Write the letters *a, i, o, u.*

h☆v○e

br○e☆kf☆st

g▢ sh▢pp△ng

g○et dr○ess○ed

c☆tch ☆ b⬠s

g▢ t▢ ☆ c☆f○e

F Read and write *always, often, sometimes, never.*

✓	✓	✗	✓
✓	✓	✗	✗
✗	✓	✗	✓
✓	✓	✗	✗

1 Peter ....often....... goes to his grandmother's house.

2 Peter .... has good ideas.

3 He .... sleeps in the afternoon.

4 He..................... eats sausages for breakfast.

G *Fun at home* What do you do? Draw and tell your family.

I always go to ...

I sometimes help ...

I never eat ...

Health

A Draw lines.

1 cough

2 earache

3 cold

4 stomach-ache

5 headache

6 toothache

B Read and write.

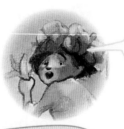 What's the matter?

1

 My nose is red and wet. I cough a lot. I've got a cold.

2

I'm tired and I don't want to listen to music. I've ....

3

 It's difficult to eat and my mouth hurts. I've ....

4

I ate lots of mangoes and fruit cakes. I've ....

18

C ▶ **Listen and colour.**
5

D ▶ **Listen again and** (circle).
6

1 Jim didn't see Sally at (school) / the park.

2 Sally has a **stomach–ache / cough**.

3 Sally is **watching TV / reading** now.

4 Sally's **nose / mouth** hurts now.

○ I can say the time.

○ I can say the days of the week.

○ I can talk about health.

○ I know some adjectives.

○ I can say what the matter is.

= 🙂

= 😐

= 🙁

Weather

A Look and write.

winrabo
....

yindw
....

nus
....

nira
....

onsw
....

dolc
....

tew
....

oth
....

B Read and write.

| wet | ~~windy~~ | warm | clouds | terrible |

1 Outside it is very ......windy...... .

2 There are .... in the sky.

3 The ground is ....

4 The weather is ....

5 Henry is in the car, because it is very ....

C Find a photo of your holiday and write.

Henry went to the countryside.
The weather was terrible.
It was windy and wet.
He liked flying his kite.

I went to.............................. .
The weather ....
It was ....
I liked ....

city

sunny

beach

mountains

cold

hot

taking photos

playing games

going to the sea

D *Fun at home* Tell your friend about your holiday.

The weather was ....

I went to ....

It was ....

21

Review

Read and write.

bed	Saturday	bat	stairs	Sunday	grandmother	earache

~~aunt~~   ~~desk~~   ~~headache~~   whale   ~~rain~~   snow
~~kitten~~   snail   rainbow   daughter   lamp   cough   uncle
stomach-ache   ~~Monday~~   Thursday   sunny

1 family
.aunt.........

2 home
.desk.........

3 time
.Monday....

4 animals
.kitten.......

5 health
headache

6 weather
.rain..........

Read about Jump and draw his crazy holiday.

Hello! My name's Jump, the alien. Last week I went in my spaceship to a strange world.
Everything was different there! On Sunday I went to school and we played outside all day because it rained.

I don't like Mondays but last Monday was fun. I played football and I got four goals. I never used my feet, only my ears. Then I went home.
What a fantastic holiday!

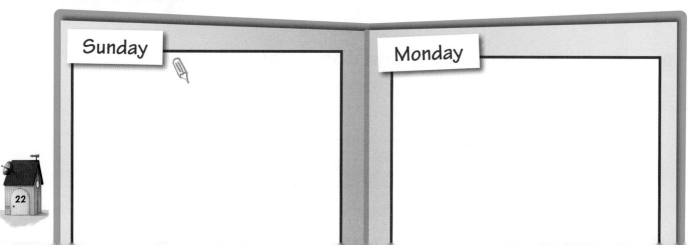

Sunday

Monday

C Read and write.

~~went to~~   saw   ate   played   was

On Monday I _went to the zoo_.................................

On Tuesday I ....

On Wednesday I ....

On Thursday I ....

On Friday I ....

D *Fun at home* **Tell your family about your best/worst day this week.**

I saw my grandmother on Friday.

○ I can read about a crazy holiday.

○ I can talk about the weather.

○ I can speak and write about my holiday.

○ I can write about my week.

○ I can speak about my day.

= ☺

= 😐

= ☹

Let's have fun!

Fun at home Ask and answer the questions. Make a video.

- What's your name?
- My name is Paul.
- How old are you?
- I'm 9.
- What's your favourite sport?
- I love basketball.

B Find a picture of an animal. Read and write.

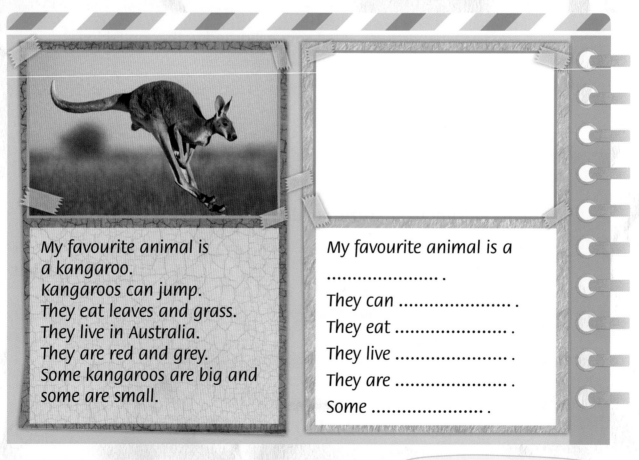

My favourite animal is
a kangaroo.
Kangaroos can jump.
They eat leaves and grass.
They live in Australia.
They are red and grey.
Some kangaroos are big and
some are small.

My favourite animal is a
....
They can ....
They eat ....
They live ....
They are ....
Some ....

Tell your family about your animal.

My favourite animal is a ...

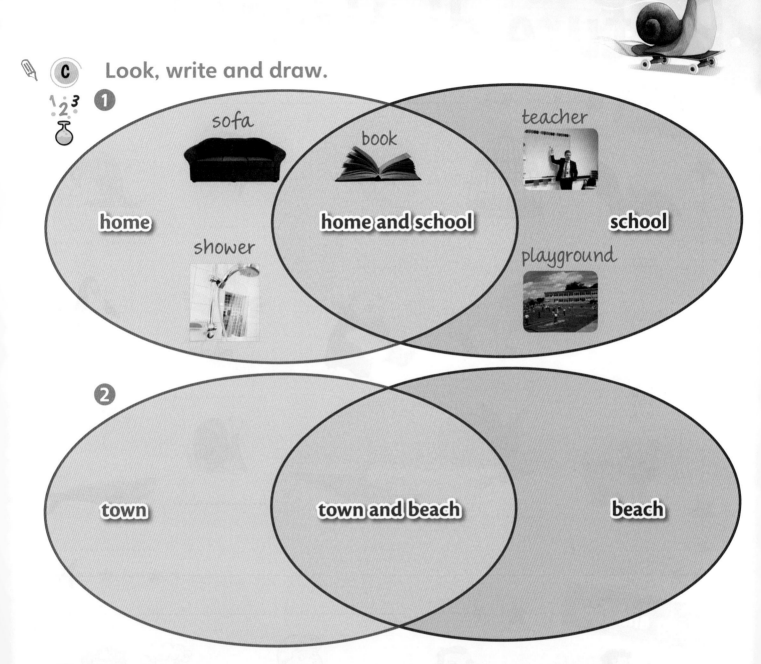

C Look, write and draw.

①

sofa

book

teacher

home

home and school

school

shower

playground

②

town

town and beach

beach

D Write on stickers and put them on things in your house.

cupboard

football

laptop

towel

homework

sweater

25

Picture dictionary

......bat......

....

....

....

....

....

....

....

....

....

....

....

....

....

....

Body and face

......back......

....

....

....

....

....

26

....

.....coat.....

....

....

....

Food and drink

.....bottle......

....

....

....

....

....

....

....

....

....

....

....

....

....

27

....

....

....

.....cough....

....

....

....

....

Home

....

....

...balcony...

....

....

....

....

....

....

....

....

....

Places

....

....

....

....

....

....

....

....

....

....

....

....

....

....

....

....

....

Sports and leisure

.....band.....

....

....

....

....

....

....

....

....

....

....

....

Transport

.....ticket.....

....

Weather

.....cloud.....

....

....

....

....

....

.....clown....

....

....

....

....

....

....

World around us

......city......

....

....

....

....

....

....

....

....

....

....

....

....

....

....

Acknowledgements

The author would like to thank her friends and colleagues at the British Council, Naples for their support.

The author and publisher would like to thank the ELT professionals who commented on the material at different stages of development: Michelle and Silvia Ahmet Caldelas (Spain); An Nguyen (Vietnam); Alice Soydas (Turkey); Sarah Walker (Spain).

Design and typeset by Wild Apple Design.

Cover design and header artwork by Chris Saunders (Astound).

Audio production by Hart McLeod, Cambridge.

The authors and publishers acknowledge the following sources of copyright material and are grateful for the permissions granted. While every effort has been made, it has not always been possible to identify the sources of all the material used, or to trace all copyright holders. If any omissions are brought to our notice, we will be happy to include the appropriate acknowledgements on reprinting.

The publishers are grateful to the following for permission to reproduce copyright photographs and material:
Key: BL = Below Left, BR = Below Right, CL = Centre Left, CR

pp. 24 (T): Sasa Dinic/E+/Getty Images; pp. 24 (BL): Tier Und Naturfotografie J und C Sohns/Photographer's Choice/Getty Images; pp. 25 (sofa): adrianwroth/iStock/Getty Images Plus/Getty Images; pp. 25 (shower): Per Magnus Persson/Getty Images; pp. 25 (book): Mordolff/E+/Getty Images; pp. 25 (playground): Peter Cade/The Image Bank/Getty Images; pp. 25 (teacher): Matt Cardy/Stringer/Getty Images News/Getty Images; pp. 25 (BL): gerenme/E+/Getty Images; pp. 25 (BR): 3bugsmom/iStock/Getty Images Plus/Getty Images; pp. 25 (blanket): Lightstar59/iStock/Getty Images Plus/Getty Images.

The authors and publishers are grateful to the following illustrators:
T = Top, B = Below, L = Left, R = Right, C = Centre

Akbar Ali (The Organisation) pp.29 (blanket); Marta Alvarez Miguens (Astound) pp.10 (skateboarding), pp.30 (fishing); Laetitia Aynié (Sylvie Poggio Artists Agency) pp.11 (ice hockey), pp.15 (asleep), pp.17 (asleep), pp.29 (centre), pp.30 (hop, net, roller skating), pp.31 (pop star, mountain, village, waterfall); Chiara Buccheri (Lemonade) pp.14, pp.15 (1-4); Ray and Corinne Burrows (Beehive Illustration) pp.9 (BL); Bridget Dowty (Graham-Cameron Illustration) pp.15 (breakfast), pp.29 (shower, stairs, bus stop), pp.31 (countryside, field); Andy Elkerton (Sylvie Poggio Artists Agency) pp.4 (fish, frog, goat, hippo, lizard kangaroo, panda, polar bear, snail), pp.12 (snail), pp.26 (dolphin, fly, kangaroo, lion, panda, parrot, penguin, rabbit, snail), pp.28 (bottle), pp.29 (balcony), pp.30 (tractor), pp.31 (jungle, leaf); Chris Embleton-Hall (Advocate Art) pp.29 (café), Clive Goodyer pp.16 (clocks, watch), pp.22 (BL), pp.28 (bowl, cup); Andrew Hamilton (Elephant Shoes Ink Ltd) pp.4 (horse); Fatemeh Haghnejad (Astound) pp.18, pp.19; Brett Hudson (Graham-Cameron Illustration) pp.10 (ice skating), pp.15 (comic), pp.30 (ice skating, sailing), pp.31 (pirate, sky); Nigel Kitching (Sylvie Poggio Artists Agency) pp.27 (back, beard, blonde, curly), pp.28 (cough, earache, headache, stomach-ache, temperature, toothache), pp.31 (island); Andrew Painter (Sylvie Poggio Artists Agency) pp.29 (circus, library), pp.30 (ticket), pp.31 (grass, river); Bonnie Pang (Astound) pp.10, pp.11 (baseball, band, roller skating, soccer), pp.12 (baseball cap, hockey), pp.13, pp.15 (bat), pp.30 (band); Esther Pérez-Cuadrado (Beehive Illustration) pp.4 (B), pp.5; Jamie Pogue (The Bright Agency) pp.26 (kitten), pp.30 (windy), pp.31 (city, forest); Nina de Polonia (Advocate Art) pp.4 (rabbit), pp.26 (cage, puppy), pp.28 (cheese, picnic), pp.29 (roof), pp.30 (party, roller skates), pp.31 (nurse, moon, world); Andrés Ricci (The Organisation) pp.27 (neck, shoulder, stomach), pp.29 (downstairs, upstairs, map), pp.30 (comic, goal, present, cloud), pp.31 (doctor); Anthony Rule pp.26 (shark, whale), pp.28 (glass), pp.30 (clown); Pip Sampson pp.11 (dancing), pp.27 (helmet), pp.30 (cook, farmer); Melanie Sharp (Sylvie Poggio Artists Agency) pp.17 (sausages), pp.20, pp.21, pp.28 (cry), pp.29 (shampoo, towel), pp.30 (rain, rainbow, snow, sunny); Simon Smith (Beehive Illustration) pp.6, pp.7, pp.15 (motorbike, park, supermarket), pp.28 (hospital), pp.29 (cinema, funfair, station, supermarket); Sarah Warburton pp.8, pp.9 (T), pp.11 (guitar), pp.15 (laptop), pp.31 (rock); Alex Willmore (Astound) pp.16 (phone); Sue Woollatt pp.27 (coat, scarf, sweater, swimsuit), pp.28 (coffee, milkshake, pancakes, pasta, sandwich, soup, tea), pp.29 (car park, farm, lift, market, sports centre, swimming pool), pp.31 (wave); Cherie Zamazing pp.17, pp.23, pp.27 (sauce).